THE
ANTIPODES

THE
ANTIPODES

ANNIE BAKER

THEATRE COMMUNICATIONS GROUP   NEW YORK   2018

The Antipodes is published by Theatre Communications Group, Inc.,
520 Eighth Avenue, 24th Floor, New York, NY 10018-4156

The publication of *The Antipodes* by Annie Baker, through TCG's Book Pro-
gram, is made possible in part by the New York State Council on the Arts with
the support of Governor Andrew Cuomo and the New York State Legislature.

Special thanks to Judith O. Rubin for her generous support of this publication.

TCG books are exclusively distributed to the book trade by Consortium
Book Sales and Distribution.

Library of Congress Control Number: 2018025840 (trade paper)
ISBN: 978-1-55936-568-0 (trade paper)
A catalog record for this book is available from the Library of Congress.

Book design and composition by Lisa Govan
Cover design by Rodrigo Corral
Cover illustration: Ulisse Aldrovandi, 1522–1605

First Edition, October 2018

For Heidi and Emily

THE
ANTIPODES

PRODUCTION HISTORY

The Antipodes had its world premiere at Signature Theatre (Paige Evans, Artistic Director; Erika Mallin, Executive Director; James Houghton, Founder) in New York, on April 4, 2017. It was directed by Lila Neugebauer. The scenic design was by Laura Jellinek, the costume design was by Kaye Voyce, the lighting design was by Tyler Micoleau, the sound design was by Bray Poor; the choreographer was David Neumann, the production stage manager was Laura Smith. The cast was:

SANDY	Will Patton
SARAH	Nicole Rodenburg
ELEANOR	Emily Cass McDonnell
ADAM	Phillip James Brannon
DANNY M1	Danny Mastrogiorgio
DANNY M2	Danny McCarthy
JOSH	Josh Hamilton
DAVE	Josh Charles
BRIAN	Brian Miskell
VOICE OF MAX	Hugh Dancy

CHARACTERS

SANDY, fifty-five to seventy

SARAH, twenty-two to thirty-two

ELEANOR, thirty-six to forty-six

ADAM, twenty-eight to thirty-eight

DANNY M1, forty-two to fifty-two

DANNY M2, thirty-five to forty-five

JOSH, thirty to forty

DAVE, thirty-five to forty-five

BRIAN, twenty-two to thirty-two

I worked off the assumption that both Eleanor and Adam were hired due to pressure from HR.

A windowless room. A conference table surrounded by ten black ergonomic chairs. An enormous stack of boxes full of seltzer cans.

Everyone sits around the table, except when they are getting up to get a seltzer.

Sarah is the only one whose clothes ever change between scenes, although she is always wearing some kind of jumpsuit or romper, depending on the weather.

Sandy is always wearing a baseball cap, except in the last scene.

There are a lot of hoodies and plaid shirts. Everyone is wearing an ID on a lanyard around his/her neck, except Josh.

Brian is taking notes on his laptop throughout the play, except during breaks and when he thinks Adam, Eleanor or Josh is saying something dumb.

Most of the time, the play moves at a fairly fast clip.

* indicates a leap forward in time. This leap forward should be indicated by subtle shifts in actor behavior and movement and without lights or sound.

/ is an interruption and indicates when the next line of dialogue should begin.

SANDY
No dwarves or elves or trolls.

JOSH
Giants?

ADAM
Cyclops
Griffin

DANNY M I
Human head
Body like a goat.

BRIAN
. . . Gryffindor.

ADAM
Fauns.

DANNY M I
Werewolves. Vampires.

DAVE
Obviously we can't do werewolves / or vampires.

DANNY M I
I'm just riffing.

JOSH

Cannibals.

DAVE   DANNY M1
Cannibals aren't—   Cannibals?

JOSH

Oh right.

ADAM

Charib . . .

They wait for him, then move on.

DANNY M2

Centaurs.

ADAM

Banshees.

SANDY

(to Brian)
Are you putting this in the notes?

BRIAN

Should I start taking notes?

SANDY

You should have started taking notes twenty minutes ago.
What did we say already?

DAVE

Giants . . . Centaurs . . .

DANNY M1   BRIAN
Cyclops Griffin   Hold on . . .
Humanhead goat

ADAM

Humanhead goat is a faun.

Brian has found the appropriate webpage on his laptop.

BRIAN

Okay.

DANNY M I

Giants, Centaurs, Cyclops, / uh—

JOSH

Trolls.

DAVE

We're not doing dwarves or elves or / trolls.

JOSH

Oh right.

ADAM
Manticore.   DANNY M I
Is that something?   What?
Manticore.

JOSH   DAVE
That sounds familiar.   I don't think that's a thing.

SANDY

What's a manticore? Brian?

Brian starts looking it up.

BRIAN

Uh . . .

JOSH

Medusa! What was Medusa?

ELEANOR

She was a gorgon.

JOSH

Right. What's a gorgon?

BRIAN

Manticore: lion's body and a human head.
Three rows of teeth.
   (reading to himself for a bit)
Eats people whole.

ADAM

Maybe I was thinking
of something else.

DAVE

I've never heard of that.

On a new page:

BRIAN

. . . Gorgon. A female monster.
The name derives from the Ancient Greek gorgos which means
"awful creature."
Any one of the three sisters who had hair made out of living
venomous snakes.
Medusa was raped by Poseidon so Athena got jealous and
made her super ugly.
Der der der . . .
   (reading to himself for a while)
. . . Large gorgon eyes represented by spirals, concentric circles, swastikas, firewheels / and other images.

DAVE

Swastikas?

DANNY M I

What site are you looking at?

BRIAN

A number of scholars interpret the myth of Perseus and Medusa
as a quasi-historical, sublimated memory of an actual invasion.
   (small pause)
/ What the—

SANDY

No to gorgons.
What else do we have.

They're all thinking. Dave wiggles his sock feet, which are resting on the table.

ELEANOR

Well . . . I'm Icelandic?

ADAM	DANNY MI
You are?	You're Icelandic?

ELEANOR

My dad is.
And there's a bunch of like weird Icelandic monster stuff but I don't know if that's interesting.

JOSH	DANNY MI
Iceland. That's cool.	My sister just got back from Iceland.

ADAM

Iceland is like very hip these days.

DANNY MI

She showed me this picture that looked like a screensaver.

Sarah enters with a menu and a sheet.

DANNY MI

Like there was a rainbow and a waterfall and / like an eagle.

DAVE
      (re: the menu)
Oooh . . .

DANNY M1

It's 11:30 already?

SARAH

(to Sandy, quietly)
I thought we could start with Tanaka?

SANDY

Great.
Has everyone met Sarah?
(gesturing to Dave and Danny M1)
You already know these idiots.

DAVE/DANNY M1

(a joke from last year)
HI SARAH

Sarah puts her hand on her hip, ironically coquettish.

SARAH

Hi guys.

SANDY

And then this is . . . well the new people should just say their
names.

JOSH

Josh.

ADAM

Adam.

DANNY M2

(waving hello)
Also Danny.

SANDY

I guess you'll be Danny M.

DANNY M1

But I'm Danny M.

SANDY

Oh fuck. That's weird. Someone needs a nickname.

DANNY M1

Flasheroo.

DAVE

What?!

DANNY M1

I want everyone to call me Flasheroo.

DAVE

Fuck yeah Flasheroo.

He reaches across the table and high-fives Danny M1.

ELEANOR

Oh. I'm Eleanor. Hi.

SARAH

Hi everyone.
So today we're ordering from Tanaka which is Sandy's favorite
but feel free to send in any requests in the future. I mean it
needs to be close-ish but this is kind of a weird neighborhood
so we're always looking for good new places and it doesn't need
to be *that* close.
Just write down what you want on this sheet and / um—

SANDY

Don't be shy about ordering a lot of food.

SARAH

Yeah. Order whatever you want and um . . . oh. Let me know if
there are any snacks you want that we don't have.

DANNY M I
You got great snacks, Sarah.

DAVE
Ehhhhgcellent snacks.

SARAH
Oh good. Thanks. I got
your favorite. We have a
lifetime supply of—

JOSH
What's your favorite?

DAVE
I'm addicted to Smartfood.

ELEANOR
Could we get green apples?

SARAH
What?

ELEANOR
Could we get green apples?
Like Granny Smiths?
And some almond butter?

SARAH
Sure. Yeah.
Um just email me about it so I don't forget.
Um.
What else.
Oh does everyone have their IDs?

*Everyone lifts up their ID badges which are hanging on lan-
yards around their necks, except Josh.*

JOSH
They wouldn't give me one.

SARAH
Why not?

JOSH
They said there was a problem with my paperwork.

SARAH

Uch.
Sorry.
I'll call them right now.

JOSH

Thanks!

SARAH

I'll be back for the food order in a minute.

She walks out.

SANDY

She's great.

ADAM	JOSH	DAVE
Yeah.	She seems great.	She's the sweetest and if you need anything she's like super helpful.

Sandy is perusing the menu. No one is sure what to do; do they keep talking while he's looking at it or wait for him? He turns a page.

DANNY M2

Sphinxes?

Sandy flips the menu around and looks at the other side.

SANDY

What's uni again?

DANNY M1	ADAM	DAVE
Roe.	Sea urchin.	Cod eggs.

> SANDY

Oh yeah.

He writes something down on the sheet of paper, then passes the menu to his left.

> SANDY

Let's see. Should I give my first-day schpiel?

I'll do the short version for the new guys.

Uh. Okay. I'm a pretty nice boss. I don't fire people. Unless they're complete assholes. You won't work past seven or on weekends. And I don't need you to say smart shit all the time or come up with the best most brilliant idea. I mean it's great if you do but the most important thing is that we all feel comfortable saying whatever weird shit comes into our minds. So we don't feel like we have to self-censor and we can all just sit around telling stories. Because that's where the good stuff comes from. These guys know this . . . I mean you guys have been through this . . .

 (Dave and Danny M1 nod vigorously)

I'd say half the stuff on Heathens was from our lives or just / stories we'd heard from other people.

> DANNY M1

More than half.

> SANDY

What'd you say?

> DANNY M1

More than half.
Of the stories.
Were from our lives.

> SANDY

Yeah even more than half.

Uh . . . what else. Brian was my assistant for a couple years and now he's in charge of taking all the notes. He'll write up

everything we say and then email it to us at the end of the day.
But uh . . . what was I talking about.

DAVE

Embarrassing stories.

SANDY

Yeah embarrassing or just . . . that's what we're here to do. Tell
a really good story. So we should feel comfortable saying whatever and not having to be PC or worry about anyone judging us
or anything like that. This is a sacred space and what we say
here obviously stays in the cone of silence.

DANNY M I

The cooo/oone

SANDY

Yeah the sacred cone.

DAVE

Remember Alejandra?

SANDY

We're not going to think about her right now.

ELEANOR

Who's Alejandra?

DAVE	DANNY M I
She was the worst.	She was this crazy / person who—

SANDY

I'll tell you about Alejandra some other time. Anyway the
point is one person can make everyone feel self-conscious or
judged and uh . . . yeah. That's the schpiel. When it's working
it's fun and it's like hanging out with a bunch of friends. And
just to remind you. We can do anything. Jeff and Victor have
given me carte blanche.

DANNY M1	JOSH	DAVE
Amazing.	Wow.	Awesome.

SANDY

The rest of the world might be going to hell, but stories are better than ever. And we've been given the opportunity to create something unprecedented.

So let's make an impact.

Let's make people feel shit they didn't know they were capable of feeling.

Let's fuck with everyone's heads and shift their relationship to space and time.

Let's make something wild and crazy but so fucking truthful that it gives everyone a new sense of empathy and commonality.

We can change the world.

He takes a couple of seconds to sip from a thermos.

SANDY

What I need from you guys is total commitment when you're here. So I'm going to ask you to turn your phone off when you sit down at this table.

JOSH	DANNY M2	ADAM
Sure.	Yeah.	Of course.

Eleanor stealthily reaches into her bag to turn off her phone.

SANDY

I want you to give yourself over to what we're doing, creatively and spiritually. I want you to listen hard and brainstorm harder and I want you to give me your craziest wildest ideas and then we're gonna distill those ideas down to something incredibly rigorous and specific.

I repeat: *we can do anything.*

A pause.

JOSH

But it's about monsters, right?
Or . . . a monster?

SANDY

Not necessarily.

JOSH   ADAM
I thought that's what—   That's what they told us.

SANDY

What I said was that there's something monstrous.
Something deformed and foreign and terrifying.
But it might not be a literal monster.

JOSH

Oh. Sorry. I / guess I—

SANDY

And it's definitely not a dwarf or an elf.

Laughter.

SANDY

Don't worry.
We've got a lot of time to figure it out.

*

DAVE

Sure. I'll go first. I basically won the lottery. I was a sophomore
and I was tiny, like five-foot-two or something, and I was dat-
ing this senior, Jessie, who was gorgeous and had these enormous boobs, I mean the biggest boobs in our school, like she
had to have boob reduction surgery in college / boobs, and—

DANNY M I

Why'd she date you?

DAVE

I dunno. I was good at baseball and I think she'd been with a lot of you know older sleazy seniors and she wanted some pathetic little sophomore to be nice to her. Which I was. I worshipped Jessie. And uh . . . let's see . . . I remember she kept bringing up sex and I kept putting it off because I was terrified—

JOSH

Aw man.

DAVE

—and I was very happy you know just to get a couple blow-jobs a week from my beautiful older girlfriend and then finally one night she kinda insisted and I remember I didn't want to be one of those guys who came too quickly so while we were doing it I went through my entire baseball card collection in my head, just like card after card, trying to see if I could remember them all, trying not to think about the fact that I was having sex, and afterwards she told me that I'd lasted longer than all the other guys she'd been with so I got to tell my friends that and I was pretty fucking happy about it.

He puts his sock feet up on the table. Adam is next. They all look at him.

ADAM

Uh . . . okay.
Mine was kind of confusing.
   (to Brian)
Are you putting all of this in the notes?

SANDY

He doesn't have to.

DANNY M I

You can always say "don't put this in the notes" and he won't put it in the notes.

ADAM

Okay. Don't put this in the notes.

(pause)

Uh actually no fine you can put it in the notes.

Yeah. Mine was kind of confusing because when I was sixteen
I kind of uh . . . I put like half of it in my girlfriend after junior
prom.

DAVE

Just the tip?

ADAM

It was more than just the tip. But it was for like a second and it
wasn't all of it and then she was like: "what did we just do??"
and I was like: "I don't know!" and we both freaked out.

And then for the next few years I never knew what to say when
people asked if I was a virgin so of course I said I wasn't but
it stressed me out.

And then when I was twenty I uh . . . my best female friend
and my best guy friend and I got drunk at this party and then
we lay out in a field and then uh . . . we had sex.

I mean we both had sex with her.

But it was super consensual!

Super consensual.

It was her idea.

JOSH

Did you touch his dick?

ADAM

I did not.

I went first while he uh . . . you know . . .

And then I lay there off to the side in the grass while they did it.

*The ending of the story is disappointing somehow. Danny M2
is next. After a pause:*

DANNY M2

I'm gonna pass.

DAVE

No passing!

DANNY M2

I'd like to pass.

He actually looks like there is a chance he might start crying.

SANDY

Fine you can pass.

Eleanor's next. She's considering a pass.

DAVE

No more passing!

ELEANOR

. . . Okay.
Um . . .
It was actually really nice.
Most of my friends had really weird experiences but mine was really nice.
Um.
I was a senior in high school. He bagged groceries at the health food store. I actually ended up moving in with him which is crazy now when I imagine having a eighteen-year-old daughter moving in with some guy who works at the health food store but that's what I did.
Anyway it was my eighteenth birthday and it was really sweet and um . . .
    (she looks around)
I've only told this story to other women and my boyfriends.
Um. Anyway. It was great. It was my eighteenth birthday and he made me a carrot cake and I told him that night that I wanted to lose my virginity to him and he said something like "Sounds good" / and—

DANNY M I

I bet.

ELEANOR

And um yeah we did it on his couch and um . . . I was worried
it would hurt but I think I had actually lost my technical virginity years earlier climbing a fence—I had kind of sat down
on this sharp um—and I had bled everywhere but the nice
part of it was that when we had sex it didn't really hurt at all
or maybe hurt for like a split second and then I actually came.
We actually came at the same time.

Is this too much detail?

We came at the same time and I told all my friends and none of
them believed me because half of them had never even had an
orgasm and I remember thinking I was going to have the most
amazing sex life but then of course there was like a decade of
bad sex ahead of me.

But somehow it was just kind of magical with Tony. His name
was Tony.

I think maybe it was the way his penis sort of . . . bent upward?

Sandy's phone starts making a noise. He looks at it.

SANDY

I gotta get this.

He gets up and leaves. After he's gone:

ELEANOR

Was that a bad story?

*

*They're all eating Thai food, except for Eleanor, who is spread-
ing almond butter on a sliced green apple. Brian is looking
something up on his laptop.*

BRIAN

It's pronounced Kai-MEER-a.

DAVE   JOSH

No.   Really?

Brian clicks on something in the website. A computer robot voice says: "Chimera."

DAVE

Huh.

Brian clicks again.

COMPUTER ROBOT VOICE

Chimera.
Chimera.
Chimera.

DANNY MI

Okay enough.

They go back to eating. After a while:

ELEANOR

All the women in my family are a little bit monsters.

JOSH

What does that mean?

ELEANOR

Everyone has a weird thing.

ADAM

What's a weird thing?

ELEANOR

Well my sister has two uteruses and / I have gills.

BRIAN

That's impossible.

DANNY M1

Gills? You don't have gills.

ELEANOR

Yes I do. All fetuses have gills but mine just stuck around.
They're tiny.

*She pushes back her hair to show them her temples. They all lean
forward. Some of them have to kind of scramble onto the table.*

JOSH   DANNY M1

Holy shit. That little line?   Fuck me.

ELEANOR

Yeah it's just a little pocket. They get infected sometimes though.

DANNY M2

Can you breathe underwater?

ELEANOR

I wish.

BRIAN

I don't think those are gills.

ELEANOR

But why would—you think I'm lying?

Brian goes back to looking something up on his laptop.

JOSH

And your sister / has—

ELEANOR

Yup she has two uteruses. That's not all that uncommon.
And then my mom is blind in one eye which kind of makes
her a Cyclops.
And my aunt has alopecia which means she's totally hairless.

A silence while everyone eats.

ELEANOR

Are any of you cold?

They all shake their heads no.

*

Sandy reenters.

SANDY

Morning everyone.
Sorry I'm late.

DAVE

How's Rachel?

SANDY

She's fine now.
She thought there was blood in her urine but I think she just
ate a beet salad or something and forgot about it.

They all sit there while Sandy drinks from his thermos.

DANNY M I

I once had this crazy thing.
Oh man.
This is a weird story.
I once had this crazy thing that uh . . . I don't know if it was
like a male uh . . . UTI or whatever but uh . . .
Cone of silence.

SANDY	BRIAN	ADAM	DAVE
Cone.	Cone.	Cone.	Of course CONE.

DANNY MI

Okay this was in . . . I just want to say
first of all that this was in the early years
of marriage and I'm like the most loyal
husband in the world now. But right   ADAM
after Sly was born things were kind of   Oh Jesus.
weird between me and Ellen and you
know you know we weren't having that
much / sex.

SANDY

That's what happens.

DANNY MI

But more than that we were just kind of disconnected and
I felt like she hated me and okay right cutting to the chase
I started sleeping with other people. That's not true. With this
other woman. This woman I worked with. I'm going to say this
again: Cone cone cone cone.

DAVE/SANDY/BRIAN/ADAM

CONE.

DANNY MI

Anyway we were having this really hot affair but we were like,
we were friends, and we were crazy attracted to each other,
but we like both knew we weren't in love, and we were both
married, and we like . . . we like convinced ourselves that we
weren't actually cheating on our spouses or like disrupting the
sanctity of the marriage blah blah blah if we just, uh, fucked
in the ass.

DANNY MI
If I just fucked
her in the ass.

ADAM
Wow.

SANDY
This is good.
This is good stuff.

DANNY MI
So we did that. For a while.
I mean that's what we did.

DAVE
You never fucked
her fucked her?

DANNY MI
I never did.
Okay and this was the first and last
affair I ever had. So I just want to
say for the record that I have never
actually had uh vaginal intercourse
with anyone other than my wife
since marrying my wife.
Okay.
So anyway we're fucking like
once a week
Yes having incredible anal sex like
once every week or so
And uh one day I pee and it uh . . . it
really hurts. / It just really hurts to pee.

ADAM
. . . in the ass

DAVE
Uh oh.

ADAM
Were you using a condom?

DANNY MI
I. Was. Not.
Unfortunately.

SANDY
Oh boy.

JOSH
So it was . . .
what? Gonorrhea?

DANNY MI
And I uh . . . well I don't know what it was. I get so terrified
that I have an STD and that I'm gonna have to tell Ellen and

I just go into denial mode. So I stop fucking this woman at work but I also stop fucking Ellen because (a) I'm in pain and (b) I don't want to give Ellen this STD and it just starts getting worse and worse and I like, it's like peeing razors, and it's not getting better, and my dick is like . . . how much detail do you want?

DAVE	ADAM	SANDY
Lots of detail.	Depends.	Oh Jesus.

DANNY MI

My dick starts like oozing this kind of uh yellow stuff, like I'll find just like a drop of yellow oozy pus just sitting on the tip of my dick and I'm totally freaking out and I'm too scared to go to the doctor because he'll ask me about the kind of sex I've been having, and then one afternoon Ellen isn't home and I realize I haven't jerked off in like two weeks because I've been like running around behind Ellen's back and pretending I'm not in excruciating pain and anyway I'm home alone one day for the first time in a while and I know I shouldn't because I'm sore and I'll probably make it worse but . . . I start jerking off.

ADAM

Oh no.

DANNY MI

So I jerk off and then I come and when I come . . . it's the most like terrifying thing I've ever seen. I basically come blood.

JOSH	ADAM	SANDY
Auuuggh.	Noooooo.	Fucking. Christ.

DANNY MI

I come this like enormous amount of jiz and blood and pus. And it hits the shower wall and it's the most disgusting thing in the world. It looks like someone was murdered. And I run to the kitchen and I get these paper towels and I start mopping the blood off the wall and while I'm mopping the blood off the wall I suddenly realize: I feel fine. I feel fine for the first time in weeks.

JOSH

What? How / is that—

DANNY M 1

Like somehow it . . . whatever it was inside of me just needed
to come out.
I felt like TOTALLY NORMAL again.
And I thanked God and I never fucked this other woman again.
Or anyone else.
Except my wife.

JOSH

So you never found out what it was?

DANNY M 1

Nope.

ELEANOR

And your wife didn't get sick?

DANNY M 1

Nope.

SANDY

. . . That's a good story.

Pause.

DANNY M2

Yeah.
Uh.
What you said actually reminds me of this thing.

Everyone looks at him, surprised.

DANNY M2

I mean I don't know if this is totally relevant.

Pause.

DANNY M2

Well. A few years ago we went up north to my friend's house and it was really, really cold, I mean so cold we spent most days inside, but then there was this one morning when it had rained overnight and everything had kind of thawed and I went out by myself in this big pair of boots that didn't belong to me and I just walked across a field, like I didn't stay on the road, I just walked straight into a field and I realized that it was a cornfield, a muddy cornfield full of dead corn husks, and I took one of the loose husks and put it in my pocket and then I circled back to the dirt road and walked up through the fog and I found this pink rock that was beautiful, half light pink and half dark pink, and I put that in my pocket too. And when I got back home I put the husk on the counter and I put the pink rock on the counter and I forgot about them and later that night my wife saw them and she said something like: what are those and I looked and for a second I didn't recognize them because they were such muddy sort of crusty objects and inside the house out of context they looked kind of horrible. And I was embarrassed and I said: I don't know. Which was a very strange thing for me to say because I never lie to my wife and then I opened the door and I threw them out into the night.

*

JOSH

(while getting a seltzer)
What if time
What if time
What if time had two axes. Axis. Axes. How do you say that.

DANNY M2

Axeeze.

JOSH

Time had two axeeze . . . horizontal and vertical.
  (pause)
Like how do you all see time? Do you see it horizontally?

ADAM

Uh . . .
  (closes his eyes)
. . . no . . .

DANNY M2

Yeah I see it like a line. A line going from left to / right.

JOSH

Horizontally.

ADAM

I see it kind of / vertical.

ELEANOR

I see it like a spiral. Like vertical but it's . . . it's cyclical. It's
a series of loops but it's moving in one / direction.

JOSH

But from up to down? Not down / to up?

ELEANOR

Yeah up to down.

DAVE

I have no idea what we're talking / about.

DANNY M1

"How do you see Time?" I don't see Time. Time is not something you / see.

JOSH

No no no . . . but listen. Okay.
Let's say time . . .
Let's say time has a vertical axis and a horizontal axis.
It goes like this *(horizontal gesture)*
But it also goes like this *(vertical gesture)*
And let's say there are certain things . . .
Uh . . .
Certain events that if they happen on the horizontal / axis . . .

DAVE

He's lost his mind.

Laughter.

JOSH

Um Please Just Let Me Get This Out.

They all fall silent.

JOSH

There are two kinds of time. Vertical and horizontal. And if
something happens in horizontal time, it can be . . . it's not
permanent. You can reverse it. Like one of them is the time
that we think of when we think of normal time that's moving forward and you can't go back. But then there's another
kind of time and if you do something in that kind of time you
can . . . uh . . . it's more flexible.

*They all sit there, contemplating this. Josh is trying to read
Sandy's face. Then Brian types for a while and Josh tries unsuc-
cessfully not to anxiously hover behind him and read what he's
writing.*

ELEANOR

I like it.

It's hard to gauge whether or not her liking it helps Josh's case. He sits back down.

JOSH

Thanks.

Pause.

JOSH

Why do you think time is like a spiral?

ELEANOR

Because . . .
  (she squints into the air)
I guess I just see it spiraling in front of me.
Because certain things happen over again
Like certain patterns
But . . . it's always going somewhere . . . but then there are these repetitions and you always think the you in the past is stupid and the you in the present is smarter but actually you might just be in a different part of the circle and in a couple of years you'll be back at the same spot again, but just farther down. Farther ahead. So you kind of spiral spiral spiral
  (she makes the gesture again, maybe with her knitting needle)
until I guess you die.

Pause.

ADAM

. . . are you knitting?

ELEANOR

Yeah.
  (to Sandy)
Is that okay?

JOSH

You're actually knitting something?

She holds up a small piece of knitted material.

ELEANOR

It helps me think.

They all try not to laugh.

JOSH

What are you knitting?

ELEANOR

A sweater?

*

ADAM

On the other side of the world there's a monster who looks exactly like you doing exactly what you're doing wearing the exact same clothes and eating the same food and going to the same job and thinking the same thoughts except the monster is doing it all upside down and backwards and in reverse order. He's your shadow and your mirror reflection but you're his too and when the world ends we'll all have to figure out who's real and who's the copy and who's sincere and who's joking because one of you is going to Heaven and the other is going to Hell.

Sarah has come in with a menu and a lunch sheet.

SARAH

We're doing Thai again.

DAVE

Nobody order the pad see yew.

*

JOSH

Hey when are you gonna tell us your Jerry Madigan stories.

DANNY M2

Yeah you keep / saying—

ADAM

I still can't believe you knew him.

SANDY

David's heard all my Jerry Madigan stories.

Dave nods sagely.

DAVE

But I would gladly hear them again.

ADAM

He's such a . . . I watched Paragon like seven times / when
I was—

DANNY M1

Paragon's not even his best work.

JOSH

I love Paragon!

SANDY

Paragon is pretty good. All right. Well.
Jerry taught me everything I know about journeys and exploits.
Jerry taught me everything I know about feats and accomplish-
ments. Jerry taught me everything I know about achievements
and deeds. Jerry taught me everything I know about objectives
and intentions. Jerry taught me everything I know about ten-
sion and opposition. Jerry taught me everything I know about
hunches and gut reactions. Jerry taught me everything I know
about impressions and responses. Jerry taught me everything

I know about sketches and outlines. Jerry taught me everything I know about overviews and assumptions. Jerry taught me everything I know about proposals and suggestions. Jerry taught me everything I know about detours and digressions. Jerry taught me everything I know about inklings and awareness. Jerry taught me everything I know about concepts and perception. Jerry taught me everything I know about drafts and extractions. Jerry taught me everything I know about rundown and condensation. Jerry taught me everything I know about compression and concentration. Jerry taught me everything I know about reinforcement and reduction. Jerry taught me everything I know about growth and escalation. Jerry taught me everything I know about desire and inclination. Jerry taught me everything I know about fulfillment and consummation. Jerry taught me everything I know about execution and implementation.

An awed silence.

SANDY

He was a drunk and a bigot but he never held that against anyone. I started working for him when I was nineteen. I kinda became the son he never had. He loved women but he didn't want them around when he was working. He was the funniest fucking fuck I'd ever met. I started by getting him coffee and then I started taking notes for him just like Brian does for me—

Brian beams.

SANDY

—and then I became his editor and then his business partner. No one knew more about storytelling than Jerry. He could diagnose your problem in two seconds. I brought my first story to him and he took it apart like it was a broken watch and then put it back together again and it started ticking.

DANNY M2

Do you / remember if—

SANDY

He'd grown up in a poor Irish family. He had some anecdote about rats in the drinking water. I don't remember it exactly. His father was a mean bastard and used to line Jerry and his sisters up in a row and they'd have to pick the piece of wood they wanted him to beat them / with.

JOSH

(softly)
Jesus.

SANDY

He never studied with anyone. He didn't finish high school. He developed his system all on his own and let me tell you that shit is foolproof. You can apply it to pretty much anything in the world.

Short pause.

ADAM   JOSH
And is it just—   His book changed my life.

SANDY

It's a great book.

Pause. They're waiting for more.

DANNY M I

Tell them that thing he used to say about boats. And / how—

SANDY

What do you mean about boats?

DANNY M I

Like if it floats, don't . . .
I can't remember. If it fucks / or—

SANDY

Oh yeah.
   (short pause)
If it flies, floats or fucks, rent it.

Dave guffaws. Brian nods and smiles even though he doesn't get it. Adam laughs even though he's miserable. Danny M2 and Eleanor and Josh don't get it.

JOSH

Wait will you say that / again?

SANDY

If it flies, floats or fucks, rent it.

ELEANOR	JOSH
(getting it)	
Oh.	As opposed to . . . ?

DAVE

Buying it.

Josh gets it.

JOSH

Oh. Yeah. Ha.

Danny M2 still isn't getting it.

DANNY M2

Uh. Sorry guys. I still / don't—

SANDY

   (glancing at his phone)
Let's take a ten.

He leaves, texting.

*

They're all eating Indian food.

BRIAN

(looking at his computer)

Whoa.

JOSH/ELEANOR

What?

BRIAN

Guess how old the world's oldest animal is.

DANNY M1

What kind of animal?

BRIAN

Guess.

ELEANOR   ADAM

A turtle.   Turtles live a long time.

DANNY M2

A shark?

BRIAN

Well that's interesting cuz a shark is mentioned in this article.
They just discovered a four-hundred-year-old shark off the
coast of Greenland. / But that's not the oldest.

ADAM

Four hundred?!

BRIAN

The oldest animal in the world is Ming the Clam.
She's Five Hundred And Seven.

DAVE	JOSH	ELEANOR	ADAM
Ming the Clam!	Five hundred and—	Ming!	That's insane. / That's insane.

DANNY M2
How do they know how old she is?

Brian scans the article.

BRIAN	ADAM
Uh—	She told them.
Hey. She's Icelandic.	

ELEANOR
(a little absentmindedly, looking at a text on her phone)
Yay.

DANNY M2
How do they / know how old—

BRIAN
She's an Icelandic ocean qua . . . qua-hog. Quahog.
    (pause as he reads)
They counted the rings on her shell. Like a tree I guess.

JOSH
That's so beautiful.

BRIAN
    (still reading)
But . . . oh shit.
They killed her.

ADAM	JOSH
What?!	No.

BRIAN

To find out—
"Ming was unfortunately killed by researchers when they opened her shell to figure out how old she was."

ADAM	JOSH
Jesus Christ.	That is like such an example of how messed up everything is right now. That is like . . . perfect.

BRIAN

"Ming's status as the oldest animal in the world is questionable, though. One species of jellyfish is *biologically immortal. Instead of dying it simply reverts to an earlier age in its life cycle.* This means that there is no theoretical limit to its life span but also that it is impossible to verify its age."

ADAM	DANNY MI
What. The. Fuck.	Wow.

Eleanor has been texting for the past thirty seconds or so. Everyone has noticed by now and is looking at her. She notices everyone noticing.

ELEANOR

Hi. Yeah. I know I'm being bad. I'll put it away in a second. It's my mom.
It's not like fun texting.

She finishes writing a text and puts the phone in her bag. Then she takes out a hard-boiled egg and starts shelling it.

ELEANOR

She's the worst.
She's just like gotten it into her head that my brother and I have to get all our stuff out of her basement. It's not like she's moving or anything. But what she doesn't understand is *we* don't

have basements. *We* don't have houses with basements to put all our boxes in. So if she wants to get rid of all our childhood drawings and papers and toys she's going to have to just throw them away.

Pause.

DAVE

Sooo I do just want to say for the record that Sandy's super not into people texting when we're around the table.

ELEANOR

I know. / I just—

DAVE

Like if you want to send a text you should probably just pretend you need to go to the bathroom and then / do it in there.

ELEANOR

But he's not here right now.

DAVE

I know but he could *(he glances behind him)* walk in at any moment and anyway it's sort of an honor system thing. It's about vibes in the room and keeping things / really—

ELEANOR

But he texts.

DAVE

Well. Obviously.
But he / wants us to—

ELEANOR

No I get it it was just a weird thing with my mom I won't do it anymore.

They all watch Eleanor shell her egg for a while.

DANNY M I

That smells like farts.

ELEANOR

It does?
(she smells it)
It smells like egg.

DAVE
Eggs smell like farts.

JOSH
Eggs have kind of a farty smell.

She smells it again.

ELEANOR

. . . Maybe.

She bites into the egg.

*

Sarah enters.

SARAH

Morning everyone!

A chorus of tired "mornings" in response.

SARAH

Sandy's running a little late but he should be here any minute.
(to Josh)
I have one more thing for you to sign.

JOSH

Really?

SARAH

I know.
I think we're really close though.

She hands him a packet with lots of little sticky tabs where he should sign.

JOSH

What is this?
Did they all have to sign this?
Did you all have to sign this?   SARAH
Wait, what is it?   It's a nondisclosure
                                      agreement.

SARAH

It's a nondisclosure agreement.

JOSH

But I already signed a nondisclosure agreement.

SARAH

This is a different—like a / supplemental—in case

ELEANOR
(looking at it)
I don't remember signing anything like this.

SARAH

Yeah yeah I think just when the system gets um . . .

Josh has given up and is signing it. Sarah watches him nervously.

SARAH

. . . when it doesn't recognize somebody they get a little suspicious and then there's a lot more paperwork.

He hands it back to her.

                                SARAH
Great thank you.

                                JOSH
Do you know when I'm gonna get my ID?

Sarah leaves, seeming not to hear him.

                                ADAM
Have you still not gotten paid?

Josh shakes his head no. Sandy enters, finishing a text.

                                SANDY
Hey everyone.

DAVE   JOSH   DANNY MI   ADAM
Hey.   Hi.   G'morning.   Hey.

                                SANDY
Sorry I'm late.
Rachel's dealing with another medical thing.

JOSH   ELEANOR   DAVE
Oh no.   Poor Rachel.   Is everything okay?

                                SANDY
Yeah she's fine.
Her ovary just tied itself in a knot and then it exploded.

ADAM   ELEANOR
Whoa!   Oh no!

                                SANDY
It sounds worse than it is.
She'll be fine.

Sandy sits and unscrews the lid of his thermos and thinks for a few seconds. Then:

SANDY

Worst thing that ever happened to you.

Pause.

DAVE

Sure. I'll go.
My dad shooting himself in the face.

DANNY M1

Wait, really?

ELEANOR

Oh my god.

DAVE

   (to Danny M1)
You know this story.

DANNY M1

I don't think I do.

DAVE

My mom's mom died that way too. / I told you this.

JOSH

That's awful.

DANNY M1

I don't think you did.

Dave rolls his eyes and sucks on a toothpick.

DAVE

My mom's mom shot herself in the face when my mom was seventeen and my mom was the one who found the body. Flash forward thirty years and I'm in high school and my mom wants to leave my dad because among other things he's schizophrenic although she knew that when she married him so I don't get what the big surprise is but anyway she wants to leave him after twenty years of marriage and he totally loses his shit and he makes this sick threat that if she leaves him he'll kill himself the exact same way her mom did. And she's like—long story short she doesn't take him seriously and she packs up all her shit and goes to a motel for the weekend. And then she comes back to the house to visit me but I'm staying at my uncle's and she walks into the living room and what do you know my dad has kept his word and shot himself in the fucking face and my mom relives the same trauma all over again and checks herself into an institution and meanwhile no one's thinking about me but again that's no surprise because no one was really thinking about me in the first place.

(to Danny M1)
Does it sound familiar now?

DANNY M1	JOSH
Maybe.	Dave. I'm so sorry.

DAVE

No no no no no pity parties it made me who I am and it made me want to tell stories and I ended up living with my uncle and he was the one who introduced me to Stargazer and everything else Sandy did and that was what got me to move out of my shitty town and come here and find Sandy and it gave me the hunger and the bravery to do that and now I've got a great job and a decent apartment and a beautiful girlfriend who's like a normal really sweet person and I never have go back there again or talk to any of those people so ultimately as fucked up as it sounds I'm thankful.

(to Sandy)
So I guess maybe it's the worst thing and the best thing.

Dave puts his sock feet up on the table.

SANDY

Biggest regret.
Danny.

DANNY M1

Let's see. Biggest regret.
I guess I / always—

SANDY

Not you Flasheroo.
The other Danny.

Pause.

DANNY M2

Oh.
Me?
Sorry. /
I get—

SANDY

Biggest regret.

Pause.

DANNY M2

Huh.
Let me think.
   (long pause)
Well. Uh. This one summer when I was a teenager I lived on
a farm. And I had a lot of little jobs but one of them was putting the chickens to bed at night. There were a lot of foxes
roaming around so it was important to get all the chickens
in their little chicken house by sundown and lock the door
behind them and then turn on the electric fence. And most
of the chickens would be in the chicken house already by the
time it got dark and they'd be sleeping or sleepy and I gotta

tell you there's nothing cuter than a bunch of sleepy chickens nestled up together all plump with their eyes drooping shut. But uh . . . yeah. There would usually be a few stragglers still wandering around and the guy who gave me the job told me that I was supposed to pick those stragglers up and put them in the chicken house. But for some reason I was terrified of picking up a chicken. I loved them but the idea of grabbing them and . . . I don't know I pictured them pecking me and or clawing me or me accidentally hurting them . . . maybe part of it was that I actually wanted to pick the chickens up very badly . . . there was something about their chests, those fluffy alive chicken breasts, and I loved the idea of holding them firmly but lovingly in my hands but I just couldn't picture it going the right way . . . like how to do it . . . and I worried I would hurt the chickens or be hurt by the chickens so I actually would just wait until way after sundown, like 10:30, 11 P.M., and that's when I would go lock the chicken house door and turn on the electric fence and by that time all the chickens had gone in the house and fallen asleep on their own. But I was really playing with fire because the fox could have come around before then. I mean something really bad could have happened in that two-hour window. But I was so scared of picking up a chicken that I . . . I didn't tell anyone and I took that risk every night. Luckily no chickens died that summer. But they could have.

(pause)

So I guess my regret is that I didn't ask for a . . . that I didn't just ask someone to give me a tutorial on how to hold a chicken.

Pause.

ADAM

That's / your greatest—

ELEANOR

But nothing bad happened.

DANNY M2

But it could have.
And I guess . . .
  (pause)
I guess what it's about is this sense I've always had that there's
some secret, that there's some thing in this life I don't fully
have access to, maybe it's a specific kind of joy, I'm not sure.
And that summer with the chickens I really do feel like if
I had just picked them up something would have changed in
me and my life might be very different now.

*No response from the group. He shakes his head and looks down
at his hands for a while.*

DANNY M2

Uh
Sorry
I feel like I should say something.

They all look at him. He's still looking at his hands.

DANNY M2

I really heard what you said on the first day about our stories—
about our personal stories being the material for—being part
of the inspiration for the work—
I really understand that. I think.
But uh—
Sometimes when I tell personal stories to you guys
Like just now
It doesn't feel real.
It feels misleading.

Pause.

SANDY

. . . What do you mean misleading.

DANNY M2

Afterwards I feel like I made something up. Even though I didn't.

There's not enough context or—

I'm telling a story because I think you want me to tell a story.

And then I'm trying to figure out how you all see me in relation to the story.

And I can tell the way you're seeing me is not the way I am.

Pause.

DANNY M2

It just gets so personal.

And I guess I've always felt like my personal life is the part of my life that I don't want to turn into a story.

   (long pause)

I also just want to add that I feel really lucky to be here and I really respect everyone in this room.

And I really respect what we're doing.

Silence. The only movement is Dave transferring his toothpick from one side of his mouth to the other and then back again. It seems like Sandy might say something. Then, after a long while, he starts texting. Then he dials a number. Then he strolls out of the room.

DAVE

. . . I guess we're on a ten.

Eleanor takes out an egg and starts shelling it.

BRIAN

   (looking at his laptop)

Did you know that a whale off the coast of Brazil can hear what another whale is saying off the coast of Alaska? Something about the way the ocean transmits sound.

ADAM

I like that.

BRIAN

So if you're a whale you're hearing like every other whale in
your hemisphere all talking at the same time. I mean not talking. Making / whale—

Sarah sticks her head in.

SARAH

Hey um Danny M?
Danny M Two?
Sandy was wondering if he could talk to you in his office for
a second.

Pause.

DANNY M2

Yeah.
Yeah of course.

*He exits, never to return. They all sit there, worried, except for
Dave, who is throwing pieces of Smartfood up into the air and
catching them in his mouth.*

*

Sandy's back.

ELEANOR

And so the only way to kill the monster is to find his heart. But
his heart is on an island on the other side of the world. And
on that island there's a church and inside that church there's
a well and inside that well there's a duck and inside that duck
there's an egg and inside that egg is his heart. So if you enter
his cave you're probably not gonna make it out alive.

ANNIE BAKER

*

JOSH

Imagine a world like ours.
With clocks and calendars.
But all the clocks tell a different kind of time.
You know how there are certain insects
And they only live a couple of days
But those days must go by so slowly, you know?
Because they're like literally a lifetime!

DANNY MI   DAVE
Yeah.   . . . Okay.

JOSH

So imagine a world like ours but the time the clock is telling
is . . .
Well so a day could actually be a century. Like the clock face
is measuring years.
Or it could be the opposite and an hour on the clock or what
looks like an hour on the clock is actually a second. Or a
millisecond.
So it's a totally different world but it appears the same. But to
them a millisecond is a lifetime. / Or a hundred years is a minute.

ELEANOR

Ooh that just gave me tingles.

ADAM

Do you guys know about the yugas?

They all shake their heads no, except Eleanor.

ADAM

It's this Hindu cyclical idea of time and the universe and the
idea is that we're always in one of four ages. Yugas. And when
you're done with the fourth yuga you cycle back to the first.

54

And each yuga is like hundreds of thousands of years long
and each one is worse than the one that came before. Like
right now we're supposedly living in something called the Kali
Yuga which is the most like demonic fucked-up age you can
be in. And at the end of this yuga the universe will return to
some like primordial ocean state for the length of all the past
four yugas combined and then everything will start all over
and people will be like nice to each other again.

JOSH

Yeah.
Yeah.
Cool.
I mean that's a little different from what I was saying but
yeah that's—
That's cool.
. . . So what I was saying was that maybe there's a world where
people are experiencing—
Their world just measures time differently.
/ They—

DAVE

How do we . . . how do we tell that story though?

*Sarah has entered with a new box of seltzer. She stacks it on top
of the other boxes.*

JOSH

What do you mean?

DAVE

If their minute is our century or our minute is their decade
or—whatever—how do we tell the story of—are we telling the
story in our time or in theirs?

JOSH

Yeah. Maybe there's a way to—
Maybe that would be the point.

DAVE

What would be the point?

JOSH

Like messing with all of that and—

*

SARAH

Oh. Sorry. I didn't realize you meant me. I thought you were talking / to—

SANDY

I meant you.

SARAH

Wow.
Um.
Okay.
I feel kind of on the spot.

Pause.

SARAH

Well. Um. Hmm.
I guess only Sandy knows this but my mom died when I was thirteen?

DANNY M I	ELEANOR	JOSH	ADAM
Oh shit.	I'm so sorry.	That's awful.	Sorry, Sarah.

SARAH

Yeah I mean it's okay. I mean it's not okay. It's super sad. But it's like my life so . . . yeah.

Short pause.

SARAH

Anyway. Um. I kind of had this crazy experience like one year after she died.

Um.

(to Sandy)

You really want me to tell them about it?

He nods.

SARAH

Well. My dad remarried pretty quickly. And my stepmother and I didn't really get along. She was kind of this—well she was like this sort of makeup-y like—she came from a lot of inherited wealth and my mom was like—she was a social worker and she and my dad were always just trying to make ends meet. And then like six months after my mom dies my dad remarries and suddenly we're like living in this big house on the other side of town and I'm supposed to be really excited about it. But it just feels—I mean the house feels big and creepy and lonely. And my stepmother already has two daughters and one of them is in college but the other one is around my age and like . . . she's this like popular girl who goes to private school and she like clearly hates me and she and my stepmother are like super girly.

Anyway.

Wait you guys really want to hear this? This isn't boring?

DANNY MI	ADAM	JOSH
No.	No.	Keep going!

SARAH

Okay well at one point my dad went on a business trip and I was alone with my stepmother and my stepsister for two weeks. And one night my stepmother was cooking dinner and she said that she didn't have any um rosemary for this lamb stew she was making. So she told me to walk down the street and go to the little blue house at the end of the cul-de-sac and to ask the old woman who lived there if she had any rosemary we could borrow.

But I was scared. Everyone at my school said the little blue house was haunted and that the old woman who lived there was a witch. So I'm standing in my bedroom trying to decide what to do when this doll my mom gave me right before she died starts talking to me. And the doll says: "Don't be afraid. Just do what you're told but don't forget to bring me with you." So I walk down the street and it's dark and kind of creepy and when I get to the little blue house I realize for the first time that the fence which has always just seemed like plain painted white wood to me is actually made out of bones and on the top of every post is a human skull.

The phone starts ringing in the other room.

SARAH

Oh shoot.

The phone keeps ringing.

SARAH

If that's Jeff I should get it.

SANDY

Did Jeff say he was gonna call?

SARAH

He said later today or tomorrow.
   (pause, phone still ringing)
I'm gonna get it just in case.
Sorry guys.
Hold on one sec.

She leaves. They all sit there in silence, waiting. After about fif-teen seconds, she comes back in.

SARAH

It wasn't Jeff.

SANDY

Why is he calling at all?

SARAH

I think he wanted to check in about the schedule and / see if there's any way he can—

SANDY

Check in about the schedule? There's no problem with the schedule. We're on schedule.

SARAH

Great.

SANDY

When you talk to him tell him we're on schedule.
Because I don't want to talk to him.

SARAH

Great. Yeah. He knows we're on schedule. I think he just likes to feel included and so he was reaching out to see if he could help or if there's anything we need or . . .

Sandy pointedly checks his phone. Sarah stands there for a few seconds.

SARAH

Oh yeah on top of every post was a human skull. So I'm terrified! Obviously.
And yeah I knock on the door and this old lady opens it and she looks like a million years old and I ask her if she has any rosemary and she says she has to check first and why don't I come inside. And like this feels like a really really bad idea but the doll whispers to me that I should do as I'm told and go inside. And so I go inside and it's basically like my

worst nightmare. The old woman locks me in a room and tells me that she's going to put me in the oven and eat me unless I clean her whole house and separate the moldy corn from the good corn by the next day at sundown. Oh yeah she has this like enormous vat of corn kernels. Maybe I forgot to mention that. It's like an impossible task. So I'm freaking out and then the doll says to me: "Go to sleep. Morning is wiser than evening." So I go to sleep and in the morning I wake up and the old lady has gone off to do errands and my doll has already like amazingly cleaned the whole house and has separated all the thousands of moldy kernels of corn from the good kernels of corn. And when the old woman comes home that night she can't believe it and she gets really mad because she was planning on eating me for dinner. And then she gives me another task for the next day. Now I have to clean every single kernel of corn until it's shiny and bright and I have to do it before sundown. It's another impossible task since there are like tens of thousands of kernels of corn. So that night the same thing happens . . . I cry in my room and then the doll says: "Go to sleep. Morning is wiser than evening." And then when I wake up in the morning my awesome doll has already cleaned every single kernel of corn! And when the old woman gets home that evening hungry for dinner she can't believe that all the corn is clean and she gets really mad and yells: "How did you do all the work I gave you?" And I just say: "I did it with the blessing of my mother," because my mother did give me the doll and I didn't want to say, like, "The doll did it for me." Anyway right after I say that the old woman gets really scared and she says: "I don't want any blessings in my house," and she pushes me out the front door and down to the gate made out of human bones and skulls. Then she takes one of the skulls and puts it on a pole for me and says: "This will light your way home." And sure enough there's fire inside the skull and it burns through the eyes and lights my way back to my stepmother's house. When I get back home I try to hide the skull in the garbage cans in our driveway so my stepmother doesn't find out but then I hear this little voice coming out of the skull. It's saying: "Don't throw me away. Take me to your stepmother." So I bring the skull inside and it stares at my stepmother and stepsister with these burning eyes and the eyes follow them wherever they go. The eyes burn right into their evil souls. And by the next morning they had both turned to ash.

Pause.

SARAH

That's it.

Pause.

SARAH

Did everyone write down their lunch orders?
Where's the sheet?

Josh hands her the sheet.

SARAH

Lunch should be here by one at the latest.

She leaves.

*

Sandy vacates his chair at the end of the table and then they all put on tiny goggles and face the empty chair. They are talking to someone we can't see. We can only hear his voice. He has a posh British accent.

MAX

Hello!
Oh there you all are!

DAVE	ADAM	DANNY MI	JOSH	ELEANOR
Hi	Hello	Hey!	Hi	So nice to meet you!

SANDY

Why don't you all introduce yourselves.

DAVE

Hey Max. You know me.
  (pause)
/ Dave.

MAX

Yes hello Dave!

DANNY MI

Danny. / We—

MAX

Yes Danny I remember Danny hello.

JOSH

Josh.

ADAM

Adam.

ELEANOR

Eleanor.

BRIAN

Brian.

Pause.

MAX

Brilliant. Hello everyone.

SANDY

This is the team, Max.

MAX

Yes yes *(garbled)* great and it's a *(garbled)* in every way.

They all smile at Max, trying to decide whether or not to say something to him about the connection. Sandy gives Brian a look like "fix this."

SANDY

How are you, Max?

MAX

I'm doing quite well. I'm sitting here in my kitchen and it's finally sunny after a few days of clouds and I'm very happy to talk *(garbled)* all of you.

Brian exits to go find Sarah.

SANDY

We're really happy to talk to you too.
You've got a lot of big fans in this room.

Danny M1 nudges or winks at Eleanor. She mouths "stop!!"

MAX

Well you already all know how *(garbled)* you are to be working with Sandy and I just want to say Sandy how lucky *I* feel to be embarking on em another journey with you. Heathens was such a success in every way, ah, artistically, financially, *(garbled)* we're thrilled you want to make something else with us.

SANDY

I'm thrilled too.
I'm thrilled too.

Brian and Sarah reenter and start scrambling around for a solution to the bad connection without Max seeing them.

MAX

(garbled garbled) so just wanted to check in with what you all are thinking. I obviously want to give you a lot of *(garbled)* but we're all eager to know what you're cooking up in that *(garbled)*.

SANDY

Well Max it's only been what five, six weeks, so we've been doing a lot of talking, a lot of getting to know each other, you know how I like to break everyone down and make them tell me stories from their childhood / and—

MAX

(garbled garbled)

SANDY

Yup. Yup.
And we're also asking each other big questions about time and space and the nature of what we all do for a living, you know?

MAX

(chuckles)
Yes. Sounds very *(garbled)*.

Brian and Sarah somehow communicate to Sandy that the problem is not fixable. Sarah exits. Sandy stoically launches into his pitch.

SANDY

So we're asking questions like:
What would communication look like without time?
(pause)
Does God think in generals or particulars?
(pause)
What if effects came before causes and answers before questions?
(pause)

Can you have meaning without matter?

Because we've been talking about the fact that whales and dolphins are telling each other stories all the time but they're doing it without words or pictures or objects.

What if we could do that for this project, Max?

What if we could tell the story that's the only story we all need to know?

And we didn't even have to write it down or turn it into code or hire actors?

If you think about the greatest thinkers in world history

Jesus

Socrates

Confucius

None of those guys recorded anything or wrote anything down.

And what we know about them we know through other people telling stories about their stories.

Could we go back to the beginning?

Could we remake our collective unconscious?

Nothing from Max. Maybe a little static.

SANDY

And Dave had this—

Dave why don't you tell him.

Pause.

DAVE

Really?

SANDY

Yeah yeah. Go ahead.

Dave wishes he'd been prepared for this life-changing moment but he jumps in anyway.

DAVE

Well Sandy can tell you I see everything, including time, in terms of circles and spirals. In terms of loops. I'm the loop guy.

(Eleanor looks at him, betrayed, but then quickly goes back to Max)

And so Sandy and I have been talking about a story that's a kind of ouroboros. A snake eating its own tail. So there's a point at which, without realizing it, you come back full circle and—picture this visual—you actually encounter yourself but from behind. Picture taking a hike and thinking you've walked in a straight line but then suddenly you find yourself back where you started and you're staring at your old self, the self who stood there at the beginning of the hike, tying his shoe-laces, but you're looking at the back of his head.

Still no response from Max.

SANDY

You still there, Max?

MAX

Yes. Yes. Although I think you lost me when you *(garbled)* talking about snakes eating their own tails.

Max chuckles.

SANDY

Forget about that, Max. That's not the important part.

Dave scoots back in his chair, cowed.

MAX

(garbled garbled) . . . heady stuff.

SANDY

Mmhm.
Say that again?

MAX
It sounds like you're getting into *(garbled garbled)* stuff.

SANDY
Yeah. Yeah. We are.

MAX
But ultimately you know what we love about you is your ability to just tell a really simple *(garbled)*, to reel people in and make them *(garbled garbled)*.

SANDY
Sure, sure.

A long silence.

MAX
. . . Well. You seem like a lovely group.

JOSH   ELEANOR   ADAM
Yeah.   You too!   Thanks so much.

MAX
I'm going to sign off now because the dog is looking a bit anxious and pawing at the back door and I think he needs to take a wee.

SANDY
Thanks for listening, Max.

MAX
Thank you *(garbled)* everyone.

JOSH/DANNY MI/ELEANOR/ADAM
Bye/Bye/Thank you!/Nice meeting you.

Whatever they've been looking at disappears. They all take off their goggles.

JOSH

Well that was pretty cool.

ADAM

I can't believe that was / him.

ELEANOR

He looks so old.

JOSH

I thought he looked great.

ELEANOR

Yeah but he used to be so sexy.

DANNY M I

He's still a good-looking guy.

ELEANOR

Yeah but he's clearly had a face-lift.

JOSH

He has not had a face-lift.

ELEANOR

Yes he has! Yes he has! Oh my god men can never tell.
He's had his eyelids done and his face lifted and they shaved
away some of his chin and those are hair implants.

ADAM

You're insane.

ELEANOR	JOSH
I would bet you a million gazillion dollars.	He hasn't had plastic surgery. That's so not his style.

SANDY

Can everyone please just be quiet for thirty seconds so I can
hear myself think?

They sit in silence.

*

SANDY

Where do I begin.
Well first of all the things she said never had anything to do
with the things we were talking about. We'd be breaking a
story and Alejandra would say: out of nowhere: she'd say uh
did anyone know there's a solar eclipse tomorrow or or have
you heard / about the war in—

DANNY MI

She had insane dietary restrictions. But not just about what she
ate.
Like she couldn't be in the same room as certain, uh— / what
was—

SANDY/DAVE

Barbecue sauce.

DANNY MI

Yeah she couldn't be in the same room as barbecue sauce!

DAVE

Once I had barbecue sauce on my sandwich and she smelled
it and ran like puking to the bathroom.

DANNY MI

How many sick days did she take?

SANDY

Uh . . . thirteen? Fourteen?

DAVE

She was gone at least one day every week with some crazy mysterious illness so then when she came back we'd have to spend an hour filling her in.

DANNY M I

Everything offended her.

DAVE

Everything offended her.

DANNY M I

She would just say about everything: "That's offensive."

DAVE

No, remember, she would say: "I'm sorry, that's—"

DANNY M I

Do / her—

DAVE

"I'm sorry, but that's offensive."

DANNY M I

That's what she sounded like.

SANDY

She knew I couldn't fire her. She made it clear that if I fired her she'd start trouble.

DAVE

But she was also in love with Sandy.

SANDY

I don't know about that.

DANNY M I

She was *in love* with Sandy.

SANDY

She was always offended but she was also always flirting with everyone.

DANNY MI

She would talk about how she was unhappy in her marriage. She would say it point blank. We'd all get here in the morning and she'd say I'm thinking of leaving my husband. / Just like that.

DAVE

And we're all putting up with her craziness. Like okay, whatever, this woman is crazy but we're just gonna put up with it and not say anything.

DANNY MI

AND THEN

SANDY

And then
HR calls.

DAVE

It was so bad.

SANDY

One day HR calls and says: "Someone in the room is feeling uncomfortable."
Someone is feeling like it's a hostile work environment.
Yeah.
That was the phrase.
Hostile Work Environment.
And I was like: uh, is it Alejandra? Because she's always bitching about how offensive everything is.
And they say they can't answer that question.
So the next morning when everyone gets here very politely I'm like:

Uh, look guys, I got a call from HR, and they say one of you is saying it's a hostile work environment, let's talk about it, let's just be direct and talk about it right now as a group and we'll figure it out and make it less hostile! So just speak up and tell me what's bothering you and we'll talk about it.

Pause.

SANDY

And no one says anything.
Everyone's just looking at me. Including / Alejandra.

DAVE

Most awkward moment ever.

SANDY

And I say again: let's talk about it. Just tell me what's bugging you, I say. And I make direct eye contact with her.
And she says nothing.
She just stares at me.
And I'm like, okay, well unless someone says something to my face right now I'm gonna assume we're all happy clams and please for fuck's sake don't go ratting on me to HR. If you have a problem, come talk to me.
(The same goes for all of you by the way)

DANNY MI   JOSH
Yeah.   Of course.

SANDY

I'm a nice guy. I can take it.
Just don't rat me out.

Pause.

DANNY MI

AND THEN

SANDY

And then
The next day
She doesn't show up.
She just doesn't come in.
And I assume she's sick because she's always sick.
But usually she calls Sarah to tell her.
But this day she doesn't call and no one has any idea where
she is.
So Sarah calls her cell.
And there's no answer.
And we're like okay, weird, fine, she'll just show up late.
But she never shows up late.
And Sarah tries her again at the end of the day.
HEY SARAH.

Sarah appears.

SANDY

Alejandra. How many times did you try her that day?
The first day she didn't come in.

SARAH

Um, three? Four?

SANDY

And you sent her emails too right?

SARAH

Yeah I was really worried.

SANDY

Yeah so Sarah sends her all these nice emails—thank you Sarah
that's all—

Sarah leaves.

SANDY

—and tries her and gets no response, nothing—

Calling after Sarah:

SANDY

AND DID HER PHONE GO STRAIGHT TO VOICEMAIL?

SARAH

(offstage)
YEAH.

SANDY

And her phone goes straight to voicemail.
And we're all like, well, weird, and my first thought is maybe she decided to quit after I made my little speech which honestly was a relief to me since she put such a huge damper on the creative vibes in the / room—

DANNY MI

A *huge* damper.

SANDY

—and there was no way I could have fired her without getting in trouble so I think, well, okay good, this job wasn't for her, maybe she's gonna you know amicably quit, and then a few hours later we get this panicked call from Jeff and I'm suddenly worried she's suing me for sexual harassment or something crazy and then Jeff says Alejandra's husband is wondering where she is because she didn't come home the night before.

A dramatic pause.

ADAM	ELEANOR	JOSH
What?!	That's . . .	. . . So then?

SANDY

And then these calls from Alejandra's extended family start coming in.

She's gone.

No one has any idea where she is.

Pause.

ADAM

And / then—

SANDY

That's it.

She disappeared.

She never came back.

ADAM   JOSH

What?   That's so horrible.

DANNY MI

She evaporated.

ELEANOR

Was she murdered?!

SANDY

No one ever found any evidence of it.

No body.

DAVE

I think she just took off.

She was batshit crazy and then she took off.

DANNY MI

Also remember how she was obsessed with Bora Bora?

DAVE

Yeah maybe she's like sitting on a beach in Bora Bora.

Pause.

SANDY

And later I said to Jeff: this is why you shouldn't make me hire a woman or a . . . or a Chinese person or whatever unless I meet that person and want to hire them. Don't strong-arm me into hiring people I don't want to hire.
Because they could turn out to be crazy and that doesn't do any of us any good.

Sarah appears.

SARAH

Sandy?

SANDY

Don't tell me it's Jeff.

SARAH

It's Victor.

SANDY

What does Victor want?

She doesn't say. This is for Sandy's sake.

SANDY

Yeah okay.
   (to the group)
Give me five minutes.

He leaves.

*

They've been waiting for a while.

ELEANOR

What time is it?

BRIAN

8:45.

JOSH

I thought he said we were never gonna work past seven.

ADAM

I had dinner / plans.

DANNY M I

It's not a big deal. Once on Heathens we were here until three in the morning.

DAVE
(ostensibly to the group but actually to himself)
This is a great job, you guys.
A lot of people would kill to have this job.

Pause.

ELEANOR

I miss Danny.
The other Danny.

JOSH

Has anyone talked to him?

They all shake their heads no.

ELEANOR

I liked him.

JOSH

Me too.

ADAM

I liked him but I wouldn't say I miss him.

Eleanor takes out a bottle of probiotics and swallows one with seltzer. They all watch her. Then:

ELEANOR

Anybody want a probiotic?

JOSH   DANNY MI
Yeah.   Sure.

She hands out probiotics. They all take one except for Dave. She offers the bottle to Brian. He shakes his head no. While the rest of them swallow their probiotics:

ADAM

You know what I think would be cool?

If we could—I mean science must be able to—there's got to be a way to just like attach electrodes to people's brains and stimulate the parts of the brain that respond to story and like specific story elements.

So you could make people feel all the things they would feel during a romance or an adventure or a happy ending and there would still be an art to it because you'd be figuring out which synapses to stimulate when and for exactly how long.

But the whole thing where we have to make up some fictional world or some fictional series of events or narrative concepts would be over.

And if you wanted to do something new it would just be coming up with a new um algorithm. A new sequence.

Which is really what it is anyway.

We all pretend there's something magic about it but actually it's just algorithms.

JOSH

You don't really think that.

ADAM

I do.
I think it would be such a relief.
Don't you?

*

SARAH

Morning everyone!

DANNY MI/JOSH/ELEANOR/ADAM

Morning.

SARAH

Um. Sandy's sorry but he's not gonna be able to come in today.
He had another emergency conference call with Jeff and Victor last night and he's exhausted. But he says you guys should keep um spitballing without him and he's excited to hear what you've come up with tomorrow.

ADAM

Why was it an emergency conference call?

SARAH

It wasn't.

ADAM

You just said it was an emergency conference call.

SARAH

I did?

They all nod.

SARAH

I don't know why I said that.
That's so strange.

She leaves.

*

ADAM

What do you mean by that?

DANNY M I

Sometimes certain stories
I mean Sandy's a genius
But sometimes not all his stories work out.

JOSH

But what does that mean?

DANNY M I

Sometimes they get canceled. Or sometimes he pulls the plug
on / them.

ADAM

Pulls the plug?

DANNY M I

Sometimes he realizes the idea isn't right or the room isn't right
and he pulls the plug.

ELEANOR

Were you in a room that the—where the plug got pulled?

He shakes his head no.

DANNY M I

But the room before my first room with him was brutal.
I shouldn't be talking about this.
Almost everyone was fired. And then he pulled the plug.
    (to Brian)
You were the Sarah to that room, right?

Brian nods.

ADAM

How do you know if he's gonna pull the plug? Are there warning signs?

BRIAN

Uh . . . well he usually just stops coming in.
(as they react)
This is different though.

JOSH

What happens if you're not fired but he pulls the plug?

DANNY MI

You go home.

ELEANOR

You still get paid?

DANNY MI

You go home and you still get paid.

ELEANOR

That sounds nice.

DAVE

(who has grown increasingly frustrated throughout this conversation)
It's not nice. Are you kidding? It means the room was a failure.
It means you were all working together for months for nothing.
It means you wasted Sandy's time.
It means you wasted everyone's time.
We're all so lucky to be here.
It took me years of work to get here.
And I'm not interested in wasting time.

*

SARAH

Hey guys Sandy feels terrible about this but it's the twins' birthday today and they're having a treasure hunt with over a hundred kids and Rachel still isn't feeling well so he's not gonna be able to make it in. He says to tell you—

*

SARAH

Hey guys I have really sad news.
Sandy's therapist died.

ADAM	ELEANOR	JOSH
Oh no	Oh my god	That's so sad!

SARAH

So he's not gonna be able to make it in / today.

JOSH

Of course, I mean he / should—

SARAH

They're not sure when the funeral is happening yet but he'll know more in—

*

SARAH

Hey guys
This is my bad but I totally forgot Sandy is giving the keynote speech at this conference today. Anyway he's gonna be there today and tonight but he said to tell you to keep going and keep um breaking stories—I think he said something about breaking the story open?—and also that you guys are geniuses and he—

*

Sandy stands in the doorway, wearing sunglasses.

SANDY

Hey.

ADAM	DANNY MI	DAVE	JOSH
Hi	Hey	Sandy!	You're back!

SANDY

I've only got a few minutes but / I wanted to stop in and—

DAVE	JOSH	DANNY MI
Oh!	Aw . . .	Oh no is everything okay?

SANDY

—yeah everything's fine Rachel's doing a little better but things are pretty crazy so I gotta head home in a few / minutes.

DAVE	JOSH	DANNY MI
Of course.	Thanks for stopping by.	Please send her our love.

SANDY

I just wanted to remind all of you that what you're doing is important. We need stories. As a culture. It's what we live for. These are dark times. Stories are a little bit of light that we can cup in our palms like votive candles to show us the way out of the forest. Every single one of you was changed by a story at some point in your life or else you wouldn't be here, right? Think back to the time when you were a little kid and a story changed your life. Do that right now.
  (a pause as he waits for them to think of the time)
The stories we create teach people what it's like to be someone else on a visceral level. As storytellers we know how to shift perspective and inhabit different viewpoints. Imagine what

would happen if everyone in the world could do every once in
a while what we already do on a daily basis.
It would be revolutionary.
    (he checks his phone)
Shit I gotta go.
Stay safe in this crazy weather.

As he's leaving:

JOSH

Wait Sandy?

Sandy turns around and looks at him.

JOSH

I'm so sorry to keep you here.
But uh . . . yeah. Sorry.
It's been more than three months and I actually haven't been
paid.

Sandy regards him. Then everyone else.

SANDY

Are all of *you* being paid?

ADAM	DAVE	DANNY MI
Yup.	Yeah.	Yeah.

Nods from the others.

SANDY

Did you talk to Sarah?

JOSH

Yeah Sarah's been great. But uh . . . it's still not happening.
I've jumped through a lot of hoops and filled out a lot of papers
and uh . . . yeah.

I also still don't have my ID and every day when I come in
I have to wait in line and show my passport to security and
sign in and get my picture taken.

Pause.

JOSH

I'm really sorry to bring it up now.
I realize it's a bad time.

SANDY

I need to go deal with some stuff at home.

JOSH

Yeah. Yeah. Of course.

SANDY

Can we talk about this / later?

JOSH

Yeah. Yeah. Of course.
Sorry. I know I jumped the gun.

Sandy leaves.

JOSH

  (averting his eyes)
Sorry everyone.

*

ELEANOR

Did you fill your bathtub?

DAVE

I don't believe in filling my bathtub.

DANNY MI
What does that mean?

JOSH
I'm worried if I fill my bathtub it'll crash down through my neighbor's ceiling.

ADAM
I filled my bathtub.

ELEANOR
I bought ten almond butters.

ADAM
Do you have flashlights?

ELEANOR
I have candles.

JOSH
I bought five flashlights.

ADAM
Is Sarah still here?

DANNY MI
SARAH?

Sarah appears.

SARAH
Hi guys!

JOSH
We were wondering how late you were gonna stay today.

SARAH
I'll stay as long as you guys stay! / That's my job.

JOSH
Oh you don't have to do that.

DANNY MI
Go home and be safe!

SARAH

No way. I'm manning the phones and I'm here if you need anything.

Pause.

ADAM

Do you think Sandy would be okay with us leaving early today?

SARAH

Well I know he was hoping you guys could hang around this weekend just cuz we're behind schedule and Jeff is freaking out a little bit so it would be great to have some ideas to show him on Monday?
    (they react)
But I mean of course he doesn't want you to feel like you're putting yourselves in danger or anything so if you feel nervous about it we should probably let him know and he / can—

DAVE

Never mind. Never mind.
We're not going home.

SARAH

We can all order dinner.
I called Huey's and they're doing deliveries until nine.

DANNY MI

Great. Thanks.

SARAH

Just let me know if you need anything.
    (a pep talk)
You guys are awesome!

ELEANOR/JOSH

Yay./Thanks Sarah.

SARAH

And if it is the apocalypse and we all get stuck here we can live off Smartfood and green apples.

DAVE

And start a new society.

A small pause before she turns and leaves.

JOSH

Fuck.

ADAM

I wish I had my toothbrush.

ELEANOR

Can I make a confession?

They all look at her.

ELEANOR

I feel a tiny bit excited.

*

DAVE

There are seven types of stories in the world. Rags to Riches. The Quest. Killing the Monster. Voyage / and—

ADAM

How is The Quest different from Killing the Monster?

DAVE

You're trying to get somewhere. You're trying to get to the castle or the golden fleece and you might kill a monster along the way but the point isn't killing the monster.

. . . Rags to Riches, The Quest, Killing the Monster, Voyage and Return, Comedy, Tragedy, and Rebirth. Rebirth is about deciding to change and become a better person.

*

DANNY MI

There are thirty-six types of stories in the world.
Supplication, Crime by Vengeance, Pursuit, Disaster, Abduction, Murderous Adultery, Vengeance for Kin upon Kin, Fatal Imprudence, Madness, Self Sacrifice for Ideals, Self Sacrifice for Kin, All Sacrificed for Passion, Obstacles to Love, Conflict with a God, Mistaken Jealousy, Erroneous Judgment, Loss of Loved Ones, Recovery of Loved Ones . . .
Was that thirty-six?

BRIAN

That was like nineteen.

DANNY MI

. . . Rivalry of Superior Versus Inferior.
Ambition.
An Enemy Loved.
And Murderous Adultery.

*

JOSH

There are ten types of stories in the world. A Threshold Crossing, A Brother Battle, A Dragon Battle, Dismemberment, Crucifixion, Abduction, A Terrible Storm, A Night Sea Journey, A Wonder Journey, or A Journey into the Belly of a Whale.

*

Brian has dragged in a white board on wheels and is standing in front of it.

BRIAN

You make a sigil when just wanting something isn't enough and normal chaos magick isn't working.

Actually sometimes wanting something is bad because then you're like ego-driven and you get anxious and afraid of failure. So you have to create a symbol or a mantra that you can put all your energy into and then forget about.

So for instance let's say your wish is . . .

Uh . . .

He writes on the white board:
I WANT TO MEET A SUCCUBUS IN A DREAM

BRIAN

Then you write it out phonetically

He writes on the white board:
AI WAH NAMEEDASUK YOOBISINA DREEM

DANNY MI

Ai wah nameedasuk yoobisina—oh I get it.

BRIAN

And then you remove the letters you don't like:

He erases some letters so now it reads:
WA NAMEESUK YOOBIS M

BRIAN

And then you rearrange those letters.

He writes:
AW KUSEEMAN SOOBYIS

ADAM

Aw kuseeman soobyis

BRIAN

And then that's your finished mantra and you forget everything else.

He erases everything else.

ELEANOR

Aw kuseeman soobis.

BRIAN

But that's not our wish.

He erases it.

BRIAN

What's our wish?

DAVE

To make Sandy proud.

DANNY MI

To make a fuck ton of money.

No one responds to either of these.

JOSH

To come up with the right story.
We want to come up with the right story.

Pause. Brian starts writing:
WEE WAHNTU KUM

ADAM

Ha

He keeps writing:
KUMEPWID DARAI TSTOREE

ELEANOR

Wee wahntu kumepwid darai tstoree!

He erases some letters he doesn't like so it reads:
EEWA TUKUMEP DAR TSTOR

ADAM

. . . Eewa tuumep dar tstor.

Then he writes it again with the letters scrambled:
AWEE PUUTEM RAD TROTS

ELEANOR/ADAM

Awee puutem rad trots.

He erases everything else on the board except:
AWEE PUUTEM RAD TROTS

ADAM

Awee puutem / rad trots

DANNY M I

Awee puutem rad trots

ALL

Awee puutem rad trots
Awee puutem rad trots
AWEE PUUTEM RAD TROTS
AWEE PUUTEM RAD TROTS
AWEE PUUTEM RAD TROTS
AWEE PUUTEM RAD TROTS
AWEE PUUTEM RAD TROTS
AWEE PUUTEM RAD TROTS

Then Brian draws a little circle with arrows coming out of it.

BRIAN

That's the chaosphere.

It means when you want to tap into the powers of the universe and shake off human limitations you have to stop worrying about being nice.

You have to embrace chaos and darkness.

You have to be willing to perform monstrous acts.

Pause.

ADAM

I think I just heard the rain.

BRIAN

I don't think you'd be able to hear it from here.

*

They're all sleeping. Except Brian.

He watches everyone sleeping for a while. Then he takes an animal skin out of his bag. Maybe it's the head of a bear or a wolf attached to a skin and Brian wears it over his head like a cap and cape. Then he takes out a small thurible of red liquid. Then he steals one of Eleanor's probiotics and empties it into the liquid. Then he removes his shirt, takes out a small dagger, draws a small amount of blood from his right shoulder, and puts that into the thurible too. Then, with the tip of his finger, he writes the following symbols on his chest and stomach in red:

He does a very small and subtle series of prayer gestures. It is almost a dance, but not quite. Then:

BRIAN

There are only eighteen types of stories in the world.
First, The Void.
Then The First Void.
Then The Second Void.
Then The Vast Void.
Then The Far-Extending Void.
Then The Sere Void.
Then The Unpossessing Void.
Then The Delightful.
Then The Void Fast Bound.
Then The Night.
Then The Hanging Night.
Then The Drifting Night.
Then The Moaning.
Then The Daughter of Troubled Sleep.
Then The Dawn.
Then The Abiding Day.
Then The Bright Day.
Then Space.

He puts his shirt back on, sits down, and sleeps.

*

One distant thunderclap, then silence. Eleanor wakes up. She's a little scared. Maybe the lights briefly flicker off and then on again.

ELEANOR

(*whispering*)
Alejandra?

*

They're all awake now. Most of them are lying on the floor or resting their heads on their arms.

DAVE

Sandy says that this feeling is inevitable. Sandy says that this horrible hopeless feeling is the feeling you get right before it happens.

JOSH

How does it happen?

DAVE

We just have to resist the urge to sleep or go home and we have to keep talking and telling each other stories and eventually it'll become clear.

Pause.

DAVE

Who has a story?

Pause.

DAVE

No one has a story?

Pause.

DAVE

Please God just someone tell a fucking story.

ELEANOR

You tell a story.

DAVE

I've run out.

After a very very long silence, Adam begins to speak. It comes, at least at first, from a place of total exhaustion. He speaks slowly and without affect.

ADAM

Once upon a time there was nothing.

Just the vast depths

And the spirit of the great father alone in these depths.

He was the depths

And the depths were him.

I can't tell you how lonely it was for him

Just floating in nothingness

Alone in a silent universe.

And one day his loneliness was so acute that he grew anxious

And his anxiety created a lot of energy

Just a lot of buzzing spinning energy

And so the great father sat and he concentrated all his energy

And with that lonely anxious energy

He produced something out of his head

A being

Something alive

It sprang from his forehead

But it was monstrous

It was a giant with many heads and seven thousand tongues and fifteen thousand arms and it was stupid and angry

It was a first try

But it needed to eat

So the great father concentrated and concentrated

And out of his asshole sprang a cow

A sacred proto cow

Her name was Bessie

And she provided his monstrous child with milk.

And then one day Bessie was just standing there and she started licking some gray stones that were lying at her feet.

And lo and behold as she licked them the gray stones began forming into heads. The heads of gods.

Two brothers and a sister

And they sprang up and they looked around and they saw the nothingness and they saw their older brother, the deformed stupid giant with his thousands of heads and arms.

And they fell upon him with their divine swords and they murdered him.

And out of his dead body they fashioned the world.

His veins became the rivers

His bulbous nose became the tallest mountain

They picked the dandruff off his scalp and threw it into the sky

And it became the stars.

And the two brothers and the sister frolicked in this world that was the corpse of their dead giant monster brother

And they built a golden palace where his belly used to be

But soon they were bored

So the sister fucked her older brother and then gave birth to a wolf

And then she fucked her younger brother and gave birth to a serpent

And then she fucked the great father, which no one even knew was possible

And from this fucking she was pregnant for a very long time. It was a difficult pregnancy, it was about a hundred years long, and during it she was cared for by her sons the wolf and the serpent.

And when it was finally time she gave birth to so many babies. She gave birth to the year, and then she gave birth to the month, and then she gave birth to the seasons, and then she gave birth to the minute, and then she gave birth to the second. Then she gave birth to the day, and the night, and the days of the week, and then she gave birth to dawn, and then twilight, and then she gave birth to Time, and Death, and finally she gave birth to Disease, and she gave all of these things her breasts to suck on.

And the wolf and the serpent grew jealous of all their new siblings, who were concepts and not animals, and they grew angry at their mother for not paying them enough attention, and so they cut off her head and threw it up into the sky and that became the moon.

Oh. But before they cut off their mother's head they raped her. And before she died these tiny little fleshy creatures crawled out of her mouth.

And those were the first people.

And it's unclear to this day whether people come from wolves or serpents since the wolf and the serpent raped their mother at the same time.

And the wolf and the serpent and the brother gods and the great father looked at these two little fleshy creatures, man and woman, so tiny and vulnerable, and their hearts melted.

And they came together in a kind of truce to take care of these innocent creatures.

And they made trees

And they made edible plants

And even Bessie bore a miniature calf out of her eyeball that the man and woman could take care of and call their own

And they all built a little garden for the man and the woman, and they told the man and the woman they could stay there and be happy forever.

And they were happy.

Until one day the woman saw her older half brother the serpent sliding through the garden on his belly. And she was jealous that he could slither anywhere he wanted in the world. So she climbed on his back and she traveled with him across the entire world, through the ocean where she saw the octopi and whales, through the forests where she saw the nymphs and satyrs, to the secret place on the other side of the world where the gods had banished all the mistakes they had made. She saw people with horns and people with faces on their stomachs and women with penises growing out of their foreheads and men with uteruses for mouths. She saw creatures with dog bodies and cat heads and cat bodies with monkey heads. She saw people with feet for heads and heads for feet. She saw all these hideous creatures and she waved and smiled at them and they waved and smiled back as the serpent slithered his way around the world.

And when she returned to the garden the woman told the man about what she'd seen, about the nymphs and octopi and dog people and cat people and uterus-mouthed people, and that uh . . . that was the first story ever told.
But there / were—

ELEANOR

Hold on.
I'm so sorry to interrupt.
 (to Brian)
But are you really not taking notes on this?

Brian snaps out of his nauseous reverie.

BRIAN

What?

DAVE

Are you fucking kidding? You haven't been taking notes?

BRIAN

Uh . . .

DANNY M I	ELEANOR
Why haven't you been taking notes?!	He never takes notes when it's me or Adam talking.

BRIAN

Sorry.
I don't feel so good.
I'm really / nauseous.

DAVE

Well I don't give a shit you're supposed to be writing down everything and this is the only interesting thing anyone except me has said in the past four months.

BRIAN

(tearing up)
. . . Sorry.
I feel like I'm . . .

Brian starts coughing and dry heaving. Some blood comes out of his mouth and onto his hands.

ADAM

Jesus Christ.

He dry heaves some more and then spits something out into his palm. It's a small jellyfish or a seahorse or anemone, covered in blood.
They all sit there, stunned. Then:

ELEANOR

Is / that a—

DANNY MI

You need to go home.
Right now.

Brian just sits there.

DAVE

Go home, Brian.

Brian slowly picks up his stuff and starts to go. Then he hesitates near the exit.

BRIAN

Please don't tell Sandy about this.

Head bowed in shame, he leaves. After he's gone:

DAVE

Can you remember what you said?

ADAM

I'm not sure.
   (short pause)
I was kind of just bullshitting.

JOSH

Can you keep going?

Adam thinks.

ADAM

I guess.

DANNY MI

HEY SARAH.

*It takes her a little longer than it normally does but Sarah
appears. Slightly less chipper than usual:*

SARAH

Hi guys.

DANNY MI

What time is it?

SARAH

Um . . . it's like six in the morning.

DAVE

Any word from Sandy?

SARAH

Yeah apparently one of his houses got hit really hard by the
storm.

DANNY MI	ELEANOR	JOSH
What?	Oh my god.	That's horrible.

> SARAH

Yeah.

Really scary.

A lot of water damage and I think a trampoline blew into the ocean or something.

It's lucky they were in their other house.

Also as you know Rachel is sick but now it seems like Sullivan and Samantha have the flu and their nanny just called in sick so Sandy's gonna be out for the rest of today.

But he says he thinks you guys are gonna come up with something amazing without him.

He says he has total faith in you.

A pause.

> SARAH

Is there anything else you guys need?

> DANNY M I

Well Brian just left cuz he's sick too / and—

> SARAH

Yeah I saw him run out!

> DANNY M I

—so we don't have anyone to take notes.

Silence.

> SARAH

. . . Wait are you saying you want me to do it?

> DANNY MI

I mean if you have time.

Sarah is trying to remain cool. She's been waiting for this moment for like two years.

SARAH

Um.

Yeah.

Yeah.

If the phone starts ringing in a few hours I'll have to answer it because Jeff and Victor are breathing down my neck but yeah yeah I can totally do that! Um. Hold on. Let me get my stuff.

Sarah leaves and then comes clacking back in her heels with her laptop and sits down. She takes a moment to open a document, then:

SARAH

Um. I'm ready.

Whenever you guys are.

They all look at Adam.

ADAM

I don't remember what / I was—

JOSH

And that was the first story ever told.

ADAM

Oh yeah.

Uh.

That was the first story ever told.

But there were spies in the garden, two crows named Chewy and Cha Cha and they heard the woman's story and flew back to the gods and told them what had happened. So the gods punished the woman by giving her pain in childbirth / and—

ELEANOR

And periods.

ADAM

—and periods and they told her never to leave the garden or tell stories again. But late at night she would whisper the stories into the man's ear anyway, and soon the man and woman grew so preoccupied with telling stories that they neglected the plants in their garden. And then the gods turned their backs on humans and invented war, and watched generation after generation of people kill each other and then tell each other stories about it. And eventually the wars reached the friendly peaceful penis-head monsters on the other side of the world and they were wiped out completely.

(pause)

I guess that's it.

He is exhausted. Sarah is still typing. Ten seconds later, she stops.

ADAM

I might be able to remember the first part if I go home and get some sleep.

DANNY MI

(to Sarah)

Maybe we can take the rest of the weekend off and then show this to Sandy on Monday?

Pause.

SARAH

. . . I mean he seems pretty preoccupied.
I won't—I won't say anything.

ELEANOR

Thank god.

SARAH

Awesome work you guys!

DAVE/DANNY MI

Thanks.

*

Eleanor is wearing the sweater she has been knitting through-out the play.

ELEANOR

So her whole basement was flooded, but:
I rescued these things to show you guys.

She pulls objects out of her bag one by one and passes them around.

ELEANOR

My secret diary from when I was nine.

ADAM

It's locked.

ELEANOR

Yeah that's why it's a secret diary. See it says Keep Out.

JOSH

You could pick this lock in like two seconds.

ELEANOR

I'm not ready to read it yet. Maybe I'll give it to my daughter if
I ever have a daughter.
And then this little guy.

*She takes a tiny naked Norfin troll out of a jewelry box and puts
him on the table.*

ELEANOR

That's Elvis.
I couldn't believe my mom still had him.
This is his little bed.
I thought it would be funny to bring him in.
    (pause)
Remember?
No dwarves or elves or / trolls?

JOSH
Oh yeah no trolls.

DANNY MI
Ha.

ELEANOR
And guess who this is?

She shows them a photograph.

JOSH
Aww.

ADAM
Little Eleanor.

SARAH
So sweet.

They all pass the photo around.

DAVE
You kind of look like a monkey.

ELEANOR
I know.
This is a witch's head I made when I was six from carving an apple and then drying it in the windowsill.

She puts something kind of scary on the table.

DANNY MI
Yeeks

ADAM
That's terrifying.

ELEANOR
(taking out a pile of construction paper)
And these are the first stories I ever wrote.
Well I didn't really write them.
/ I—

Sandy enters, sans baseball cap.

SANDY
Hey everyone.

JOSH	ADAM	SARAH	DAVE	DANNY M I
Hi	Hi!	Welcome back!	Hey!	Sandy!

DANNY M I

How's Rachel?

SANDY

She's uh . . . she's okay.
  (pause)
She's having a bit of a hard time.
Uh . . . yeah.
Some intense uh female stuff.
But I think she's gonna be okay.
Our beach house is fucked though.

JOSH

We heard. That's horrible.

Pause.

SANDY

Sorry I was gone for such a long time.
It's been a wild ride.

He sits and drinks from his thermos. Then:

SANDY

You guys come up with anything you're excited about?

*They all look at one another, trying to figure out what to say.
After a while:*

DAVE

Well / Adam had this—

SANDY

Yeah it's okay.
I've been thinking—
I think, uh . . .
I think it might be impossible.
What we were trying to do.
I've been in a real existential . . .
     (he makes a gesture)
It's like my life but it's not my life.
You know?

They all just stare at him.

SANDY

I think maybe there are no more stories.
Not that we've told all the stories
Or that there are only six types of stories or something
But I think maybe it's the end of an era.
Or maybe it should be the end of an era.
Like maybe this is actually the worst possible time in the history of the world to be telling stories.
You know the uh . . .
     (to Adam)
What were you telling us about?
The different ages?

ADAM

The yugas?

SANDY

Yeah the yugas.
Maybe we have to move into the next yuga.
Maybe all this shit has to burn down first.
I think maybe this yuga can't handle another story.
At least that's where I'm at this week.

Pause.

DANNY MI

Uh . . . what does this mean?

SANDY

For what?

DANNY MI

Uh for the project I guess.
For you and for / us.

SANDY

Oh yeah well I think I'm gonna head up north for a while. We've got this great little cabin near the border. It's in the middle of a forest and the air always smells like eucalyptus. Rachel's thinking she might homeschool the twins for a couple years and I'd like to take some time off to learn qigong and maybe write my memoir.

Pause.

JOSH

And what about us?

SANDY

Oh you guys should take it easy and I'll make sure Jeff pays you for the next month or two until you find another gig.
I talked to Max and Victor and we're gonna go on indefinite hiatus.
But uh . . . yeah.
Maybe you should all think about going into a different line of work.
Until the next yuga.

ADAM

I think the next yuga is like three hundred thousand years away.

Sandy chuckles.

SANDY

Yeah. Oh man.

He rubs his eyes.

SANDY

I'm really tired.
Did you order lunch?

SARAH

Yeah there's a new Tibetan place like a mile away.

ELEANOR

I ordered yak butter tea.

SARAH

I got like a chicken thing for you.

SANDY

Great. Great.

*A pause, during which Dave summons up the courage to tell
Sandy how devastated he feels.*

DAVE

Sandy. I have to say, I'm feeling / kind of—

SANDY
(noticing the pile of paper in front of Eleanor)
What are those?

ELEANOR

Oh. These are from my mom's basement.
They were in the only box of stuff that didn't get ruined in the
storm.
I wrote them when I was four. Well I didn't really write them cuz
I couldn't write yet.

I dictated them to my mom.
I also illustrated them.
 (pause)
Wanna hear one?

SANDY

Sure.

ELEANOR

Um . . .
Let's see.
 (she picks one up and reads it)
"Once about the time a little girl, she went out in the forest.
And she always checked to there to check if anything was there.
Nothing was there, cept one day she saw a rattlesnake. So she
run out of the forest. The end."

ADAM

That's a classic.

ELEANOR

Here's the picture.

She shows them a hard-to-decipher four-year-old kid picture.

SANDY

Read us another one.

ELEANOR

Um . . .
 (looking through them)
. . . okay.
"Once about the time there was a fire in the forest and some
people was camping out. And they didn't know a fire was on,
because they was asleep. So they got killed. The end."
 *(she stops and shows them all the picture, then finds another
 one)*

Oh here's a Christmas story.

"Once upon a time"—I guess I learned how to say it right eventually—"there was a little girl and she was so happy that Christmas was coming so soon. And finally Christmas came and she was so happy when she found all her things on the floor. She had jewelry and likes and happy."

That's funny. I guess I've always liked jewelry.

(she looks up at them)

"The end."